contents

2 hints for success

To obtain results that look and taste as good as ours, read through these guidelines before you start baking.

Mixing

For best results, have butter and eggs at room temperature. Do not overbeat butter and sugar mixtures, as this results in mixtures which are excessively soft, causing biscuits to spread too much during baking.

Oven positions

Two or more trays of biscuits, or pans of slices, can be baked in an oven at the same time provided no tray touches the oven walls or the closed oven door. Leave a 2cm space around each tray to allow for proper heat circulation and browning. As you bake, swap the position of trays or pans on the oven shelves – some ovens have hot spots and rotating trays ensures even browning. As a general rule, the top half of a gas oven produces the best baking results, but in an electric oven the lower half is best. Fan-forced ovens bake and brown evenly – there's no need to swap the position of trays.

Oven trays and pans

We used aluminium trays with quite shallow "walls", so the heat of the oven skimmed freely over the biscuits or slices.

Overmixed butter and sugar (left) contrasts with correctly beaten mixture (right).

Testing if biscuits are cooked

The baking times in this book are based on a minimum cooking time. Check biscuits occasionally during baking time; opening the oven door briefly will not affect results. Biscuits may look soft in the oven, but become firmer or crisp when cold. To test if a biscuit is cooked, push it gently with your finger; if it can be moved on the oven tray without breaking, it is ready to be removed from the oven.

Testing if slices are cooked

Slices, and bases for layered slices, usually feel slightly soft in the oven but will become firm when cold.

Storing and freezing biscuits and slices

To prevent biscuits and slices from softening, cool completely before storing. Keep biscuits and slices in a container just large enough to hold them – this leaves minimal air space but won't crush the contents. To avoid softening, biscuits with cream or jam fillings are best assembled just before serving. Biscuits and slices will absorb moisture from cakes, bread or scones if stored together, becoming soft in the process.

If plain biscuits or slices (unfilled and/or un-iced) do soften, place them on oven trays in a single layer and reheat, uncovered, in moderate oven for 5 to 10 minutes to re-crisp; lift onto wire racks to cool.

All baked biscuits and slices can be frozen. However, some icings and cream fillings may crack or change in appearance on thawing. Always extract as much air as possible from the container before freezing. Two months is about the maximum freezing time. Thawed un-iced and unfilled biscuits can be re-crisped – follow the directions above.

What went wrong?

If biscuits are too hard
The ingredients have been measured incorrectly, or the biscuits have been baked too long or at too high a temperature.

If biscuits are too soft
Ingredients have been measured incorrectly, or biscuits haven't been baked long enough or have been softened by steam when stacked on top of one another to cool.

If biscuits spread on the tray
The mixture is too soft due to overbeating, or the ingredients have been measured incorrectly, or the wrong type of flour has been used, or the oven was not hot enough to set the mixture quickly.

If biscuits are too brown underneath
Trays have been overgreased, causing the heat to be attracted to the base of biscuits. Use a pastry brush dipped in a small amount of melted butter to grease trays lightly and evenly, or use a light coating of cooking-oil spray. Incorrect oven position and/or temperature could also cause over-browning, as could over-measuring, particularly with sweet ingredients like sugar, honey or golden syrup.

Overbeating causes biscuits (on tray) to spread, unlike correct mixture (on slide).

peanut butter cookies

This recipe does not contain flour. You can use crunchy or smooth peanut butter.

1 cup (260g) peanut butter

1 cup (220g) caster sugar

1 egg, beaten lightly

Combine ingredients in medium bowl.

Roll rounded teaspoons of mixture into balls. Place biscuits about 5cm apart on greased oven trays, flatten slightly with a fork.

Bake in moderate oven about 15 minutes or until browned lightly. Stand biscuits 5 minutes before lifting onto wire racks to cool.

Makes about 30

6 tangy lime cookies

60g butter

2 teaspoons finely grated lime rind

1/2 cup (110g) caster sugar

1 egg yolk

1 1/4 cups (185g) self-raising flour

1 tablespoon lime juice, approximately

icing

3 teaspoons soft butter

1 cup (160g) icing sugar mixture

1 tablespoon lime juice, approximately

Beat butter, rind, sugar and egg yolk in small bowl with electric mixer until light and fluffy. Stir in flour and enough juice to make ingredients cling together. Turn dough onto floured surface, knead gently until smooth.

Roll 2 rounded teaspoons of mixture into balls; place balls about 4cm apart on greased oven trays, flatten cookies slightly. Bake in moderate oven about 15 minutes or until browned lightly; cool cookies on trays. Spread cold cookies with Icing; place on wire racks until set.

Icing Combine butter and icing sugar in medium bowl; stir in enough juice to make icing spreadable.

Makes about 25

apple cinnamon biscuits

2 eggs

1⅓ cups (275g) firmly packed brown sugar

1 teaspoon vanilla essence

½ cup (125ml) vegetable oil

2 tablespoons golden syrup

2 cups (180g) rolled oats

1½ cups (135g) chopped dried apples

1 cup (150g) plain flour

¾ cup (110g) self-raising flour

½ teaspoon bicarbonate of soda

1 teaspoon ground cinnamon

Beat eggs and sugar in small bowl with electric mixer until mixture changes colour; transfer to large bowl.

Stir in essence, oil and syrup, then oats, apple and sifted dry ingredients. Cover; refrigerate 1 hour.

Roll level tablespoons of mixture into balls; place about 6cm apart on greased oven trays. Bake in moderately hot oven about 10 minutes or until browned lightly. Stand biscuits 5 minutes before lifting onto wire racks to cool.

Makes about 45

8 orange nut biscotti

1/2 cup (110g) caster sugar

1 egg

3/4 cup (110g) plain flour

1/2 teaspoon baking powder

3/4 cup (110g) unsalted roasted macadamias, chopped

1 tablespoon cocoa powder

2 teaspoons finely grated orange rind

Whisk sugar and egg in medium bowl until combined, stir in sifted flour and baking powder, then nuts; mix to a sticky dough.

Divide dough in half. Knead sifted cocoa into one half, divide into four pieces; roll each piece into an 18cm log. Knead the orange rind into remaining dough, divide in half; roll each piece into an 18cm log.

Place one orange log on greased oven tray, place a chocolate log on each side; press logs gently together. Repeat with remaining logs, place on same tray. Bake logs in moderate oven about 30 minutes or until firm. Stand 10 minutes.

Using a serrated knife, cut warm logs diagonally into 1cm slices. Place biscotti, in single layer, on oven trays. Bake in slow oven about 15 minutes or until dry and crisp.

Makes about 36

¹/₂ cup (110g) caster sugar

1 egg

³/₄ cup (110g) plain flour

¹/₂ teaspoon baking powder

1 teaspoon ground cinnamon

¹/₂ teaspoon ground cardamom

1 cup (150g) chopped unsalted roasted cashews

Whisk sugar and egg in a medium bowl; stir in sifted dry ingredients and nuts, mix to a sticky dough.
Divide dough in half, shape each portion into an 18cm log on lightly floured surface.
Place on greased oven tray; bake in moderate oven about 30 minutes or until firm. Stand 10 minutes.
Using a serrated knife, cut warm logs diagonally into 1cm slices. Place biscotti on oven trays. Bake in slow oven about 15 minutes or until dry and crisp; cool on trays.

Makes about 36

chocolate
apricot macaroons

¾ cup (110g) finely chopped dried apricots

1 tablespoon Grand Marnier

3 egg whites

¾ cup (165g) caster sugar

1¾ cups (160g) coconut

⅓ cup (50g) white chocolate Melts, melted

⅓ cup (50g) white chocolate Melts, melted, extra

⅓ cup (50g) dark chocolate Melts, melted

Combine apricots and liqueur in small bowl; stand for 15 minutes.

Beat egg whites in small bowl with electric mixer until soft peaks form, gradually add sugar, beat until dissolved between each addition. Fold in apricot mixture, coconut and white Melts.

Spoon mixture into piping bag fitted with 2cm plain tube. Pipe 4cm lengths of mixture about 4cm apart on foil-covered oven trays. Bake in slow oven for about 25 minutes or until firm. Cool on trays. Lift macaroons onto wire racks; drizzle with extra white Melts and choc Melts.

Makes about 60

crisp sunflower

nut bread

3 egg whites

*½ cup (110g)
caster sugar*

*1 cup (150g)
plain flour*

⅓ cup (50g) pine nuts

⅓ cup (55g) pepitas

*⅓ cup (55g) sunflower
seed kernels*

*1 tablespoon
sesame seeds*

Grease 8cm x 26cm bar cake pan, line base with baking paper.

Beat egg whites in small bowl with electric mixer until soft peaks form; gradually add sugar, beating until dissolved between additions. Stir in flour, nuts, pepitas, kernels and seeds; spread mixture into prepared pan.

Bake in moderate oven about 40 minutes or until firm. Cool in pan, wrap in foil; stand overnight.

Using a serrated knife, slice bread into very thin slices. Place slices on baking-paper-lined oven trays; bake, in moderate oven about 12 minutes or until crisp.

Makes about 50

12 macadamia and white chocolate cookies

125g butter

2 teaspoons vanilla essence

1 cup (200g) firmly packed brown sugar

1 egg

1 cup (150g) plain flour

1/2 cup (75g) self-raising flour

1 cup (150g) chopped unsalted
roasted macadamias

1 cup (70g) shredded coconut

3/4 cup (65g) rolled oats

200g white chocolate, chopped

Beat butter, essence, sugar and egg in small
bowl with electric mixer until light and fluffy.
Transfer mixture to large bowl; stir in flours,
nuts, coconut, oats and chocolate.

Shape level tablespoons of mixture into balls;
place about 3cm apart on greased oven trays,
flatten slightly. Bake in moderately hot oven
about 12 minutes or until browned lightly;
cool cookies on trays.

Makes about 40

14 hazelnut crescents

125g butter

1 teaspoon
vanilla essence

1/4 cup (55g)
caster sugar

1/4 cup (50g)
brown sugar

1 egg

2 tablespoons cream

1/2 cup (55g)
hazelnut meal

1/2 cup (75g)
self-raising flour

1 1/4 cups (185g)
plain flour

1/2 teaspoon
ground cinnamon

1/2 cup (80g) icing
sugar mixture,
approximately

Beat butter, essence, caster sugar, brown sugar and egg in small bowl with electric mixer until smooth. Stir in cream, hazelnut meal, flours and cinnamon. Turn dough onto floured surface; knead gently until smooth. Cover, refrigerate 30 minutes.

Shape level tablespoons of dough into crescents; place about 3cm apart on greased oven trays. Bake in moderate oven about 15 minutes or until browned; lift onto wire racks. Sprinkle crescents thickly with sifted icing sugar, cool.

Makes about 25

honey cookies

125g butter

2 teaspoons finely
grated lemon rind

1/3 cup (75g)
caster sugar

1/3 cup (80ml)
vegetable oil

2 cups (300g)
plain flour

1 cup (150g)
self-raising flour

1/4 cup (30g) finely
chopped walnuts

2/3 cup (160ml)
orange juice

1 cup (250ml) honey

2 tablespoons finely
chopped walnuts, extra

2 teaspoons
sesame seeds

Beat butter, rind and sugar in small bowl with electric mixer until combined. Gradually beat in oil, beat until mixture is light and fluffy. Transfer mixture to large bowl; stir in flours, nuts and juice in 2 batches, mix to a soft dough.
Shape level tablespoons of mixture into egg shapes; place about 3cm apart on greased oven trays, flatten slightly. Mark cookies lightly with

fork. Bake in moderate oven about 20 minutes or until browned lightly. Stand cookies 5 minutes before lifting onto wire racks to cool.
Heat honey in small saucepan until just warm, dip biscuits in honey to coat; place on wire rack over tray, sprinkle with combined extra nuts and seeds.

Makes about 40

16 giant orange and caramel cookies

125g butter

3 teaspoons finely grated orange rind

1¹/₂ cups (300g) firmly packed brown sugar

1 egg

2 tablespoons orange juice

2¹/₄ cups (335g) plain flour

¹/₂ cup (75g) self-raising flour

2 teaspoons mixed spice

1 egg white, beaten lightly

¹/₂ cup (40g) flaked almonds

Beat butter, rind sugar and eggs in small bowl with electric mixer until light and fluffy. Transfer mixture to large bowl; stir in juice and sifted dry ingredients.

Roll 2 rounded tablespoons of mixture into balls; place on greased oven trays, allowing four cookies per tray, flatten until 5mm thick. Brush cookies with egg white, sprinkle with nuts. Bake in moderate oven about 15 minutes or until browned lightly; lift onto wire racks to cool.

Makes about 15

florentines

¾ *cup (120g) sultanas*

2 cups (60g)
Corn Flakes

¾ *cup (110g)*
unsalted roasted
peanuts, chopped finely

½ *cup (125g) finely*
chopped glacé cherries

⅔ *cup (160ml)*
sweetened
condensed milk

150g dark
chocolate, melted

Combine sultanas, Corn Flakes, peanuts, cherries and milk in medium bowl; mix well. Place slightly rounded tablespoons of mixture, about 5cm apart on baking-paper-lined oven trays. Bake in moderate oven about 10 minutes or until browned lightly; cool on trays.

Spread base of each biscuit with chocolate. Make wavy lines in chocolate with fork just before chocolate sets.

Makes about 18

18 orange

shortbread cookies

1/2 cup (75g) shelled pistachios, toasted
250g butter, chopped
1 cup (160g) icing sugar mixture
1 1/2 cups (225g) plain flour
2 tablespoons rice flour
2 tablespoons cornflour
3/4 cup (90g) almond meal
2 tablespoons orange flower water
1/3 cup (55g) icing sugar mixture, extra

Chop 1/3 cup (50g) of the pistachios, leave remaining pistachios whole.
Beat butter and icing sugar in medium bowl with electric mixer until combined. Stir in sifted flours, almond meal and chopped nuts.
Shape level tablespoons of mixture into mounds. Place mounds about 3cm apart on greased oven trays, press a whole pistachio on each. Bake in slow oven about 25 minutes or until firm. Lift cookies onto wire racks; brush with orange flower water, stand 5 minutes. Dust cookies with extra sifted icing sugar; cool.

Makes about 40

white chocolate
corn flake cookies

2 eggs

1⅓ cups (275g) firmly
packed brown sugar

1 teaspoon
vanilla essence

½ cup (125ml)
vegetable oil

150g white chocolate,
chopped coarsely

1 cup (150g)
plain flour

¾ cup (110g)
self-raising flour

½ teaspoon
bicarbonate of soda

2½ cups (75g)
Corn Flakes

Beat eggs and sugar in small bowl with electric
mixer until mixture changes colour. Transfer
mixture to large bowl; stir in essence, oil,
chocolate and sifted dry ingredients. Cover,
refrigerate 1 hour.

Roll level tablespoons of mixture into balls. Coat
the balls in Corn Flakes; place about 6cm apart
on greased oven trays, flatten slightly. Bake in
moderate oven about 15 minutes or until browned
lightly. Stand cookies 5 minutes before lifting onto
wire racks to cool.

Makes about 30

crunchy
muesli biscuits

125g butter

¼ cup (50g) brown sugar

¼ cup (55g) caster sugar

¼ cup (35g) self-raising flour

¼ cup (35g) plain flour

2 cups (60g) Corn Flakes

2 cups (260g) toasted muesli

1 egg, beaten lightly

Combine butter and sugars in medium saucepan, stir over heat until butter is melted. Remove pan from heat, stir in flours and remaining ingredients.

Drop rounded teaspoons of mixture, about 3cm apart on greased oven trays; shape into rounds. Bake in moderate oven about 10 minutes or until browned lightly; cool biscuits on trays.

Makes about 35

vanilla

currant cookies

125g butter

1 teaspoon
vanilla essence

3/4 cup (165g)
caster sugar

1 egg

2 cups (300g)
self-raising flour

1/2 cup (45g)
desiccated coconut

1/4 cup (35g)
dried currants

vanilla icing

1 1/2 cups (240g) icing
sugar mixture

2 teaspoons
vanilla essence

1 1/2 teaspoons
soft butter

1 1/2 tablespoons milk

Beat butter, essence, sugar and egg in small
bowl with electric mixer until light and fluffy.
Stir in flour, coconut and currants.

Shape 2 rounded teaspoons of mixture into
balls; place about 5cm apart on greased
oven trays, flatten cookies with hand until
5mm thick. Bake in moderately hot oven about
10 minutes or until browned lightly; cool cookies
on trays. Spread cookies thinly with Vanilla
Icing; place on wire racks until set.

Vanilla Icing Combine all ingredients in small
heatproof bowl, stir over hot water, until icing
is spreadable.

Makes about 40

double heart

biscuits

125g butter

*2/3 cup (150g)
caster sugar*

1 egg

*2 cups (300g)
plain flour*

*1 tablespoon
cocoa powder*

*60g dark chocolate,
melted*

Beat butter, sugar and egg in small bowl with electric mixer until light and fluffy; stir in flour and cocoa. Knead dough on floured surface until smooth. Halve dough, wrap one half in plastic.
Knead chocolate into remaining half of dough. Roll dark chocolate dough between sheets of baking paper until 3mm thick; repeat with lighter chocolate dough.

Cut hearts from both doughs using 6cm cutter. Place hearts 3cm apart on baking-paper-lined oven trays. Using a 3.5cm heart cutter, cut out centres from hearts.
Place light centres inside dark chocolate hearts, and dark centres inside light chocolate hearts. Bake biscuits in moderate oven about 12 minutes or until lightly browned. Transfer to wire racks to cool.

Makes about 50

fudgy choc
cherry cookies

1¹/₃ cups (200g) milk chocolate Melts

60g butter

¹/₄ cup (60ml) vegetable oil

¹/₃ cup (75g) caster sugar

2 eggs, beaten lightly

1 cup (150g) self-raising flour

1 cup (150g) plain flour

3 x 85g Cherry Ripe bars, chopped

³/₄ cup (110g) milk chocolate Melts, melted, extra

1 tablespoon vegetable oil, extra

Combine Melts, butter, oil and sugar in medium saucepan; stir over low heat until chocolate melts, cool to room temperature. Stir in egg, flours and two-thirds of the Cherry Ripe bars. Roll level tablespoons of mixture into balls, place about 3cm apart on greased oven trays. Bake in moderate oven about 15 minutes or until browned lightly; cool cookies on trays. Spread tops of cookies with combined extra Melts and extra oil, sprinkle with remaining Cherry Ripe bar.

Makes about 35

coconut
jam biscuits

2 cups (300g)
self-raising flour

1 cup (90g)
desiccated coconut

1 cup (220g)
caster sugar

200g butter, melted

2 tablespoons milk

¹/₃ cup (80ml)
strawberry jam

Combine flour, coconut and sugar in large bowl;
stir in butter and milk. Roll level tablespoons
of mixture into balls; place about 8cm apart
on greased oven trays. Using floured handle
of wooden spoon, press a hollow in each
ball about 1cm deep and 1.5cm wide; drop
¹/₄ teaspoon jam into each hollow.

Bake in moderate oven about 15 minutes or until
browned lightly. Top jam centres with additional
¹/₄ teaspoon jam; cool biscuits on trays.

Makes about 30

yogurt sultana
chip cookies

125g butter, melted

1¼ cups (35g) Corn Flakes

1 cup (150g) self-raising flour

½ cup (100g) firmly packed brown sugar

½ cup (25g) flaked coconut

200g yogurt-coated sultanas

80g dark chocolate, chopped

⅔ cup (80g) chopped roasted hazelnuts

1 egg, beaten lightly

Combine ingredients in large bowl; mix well.

Roll level tablespoons of mixture into balls; place about 5cm apart on greased oven trays. Bake in moderate oven about 12 minutes or until browned; cool cookies on trays.

Makes about 40

twice-baked
biscuits

Baking biscuits twice allows them to remain crisp for longer.

500g butter, softened

2 tablespoons finely grated lemon rind

1 cup (220g) caster sugar

395g can sweetened condensed milk

5 cups (750g) self-raising flour

1/2 cup (100g) finely chopped glacé ginger

Beat butter, rind and sugar in large bowl with electric mixer until smooth. Add condensed milk, flour, and ginger, in two batches, beating until combined.

Roll rounded teaspoons of mixture into balls; place about 4cm apart on greased oven trays, flatten slightly with a fork. Bake in moderate oven about 10 minutes or until browned lightly; cool biscuits on trays.

Place biscuits close together on trays for second baking. Bake in moderate oven about 8 minutes or until browned; cool biscuits on trays.

Makes about 120

Flavour these cookies with any of the following: 2 teaspoons of citrus rind, 100g grated dark or milk chocolate, or 1 teaspoon of ground spices – cinnamon or mixed spice is good. Beat citrus rind into the butter mixture, but add either the chocolate or spices with the flour.

200g butter

1 cup (220g) caster sugar

1 teaspoon vanilla essence

1 egg, beaten lightly

1¹/₂ cups (225g) plain flour

¹/₂ cup (75g) self-raising flour

Beat butter, sugar, essence and egg in medium bowl with electric mixer until pale in colour. Beat in flours in two batches. **Place** dough onto a sheet of baking paper and shape into a log about 4cm in diameter. Cut log in half crossways then wrap logs separately in plastic wrap and refrigerate for at least 1 hour, but up to 3 days.

Using a sharp knife, cut log into 7mm-thick slices. Place on baking-paper-lined oven trays. Bake in moderate oven about 10 minutes. Remove from oven, stand 5 minutes; transfer to wire racks to cool.

Makes about 100

banana chip
cookies

125g butter

1 teaspoon vanilla essence

1/2 cup (110g) caster sugar

1 egg

1 1/3 cups (200g)
self-raising flour

1/2 cup (40g) banana chips,
chopped

1/2 cup (60g)
chopped pecans

1/2 cup (40g) banana chips,
extra

Beat butter, essence, sugar and egg in small bowl with electric mixer until just combined. Stir in flour, banana chips and nuts.

Shape 2 rounded teaspoons of mixture into balls; place about 5cm apart on greased oven trays. Top cookies with extra banana chips. Bake in moderately hot oven about 12 minutes or until browned lightly; cool cookies on trays.

Makes about 50

double chocolate
chip cookies

250g butter

*1 teaspoon
vanilla essence*

*2/3 cup (150g) firmly
packed brown sugar*

*2/3 cup (150g)
caster sugar*

2 eggs

*2 1/2 cups (375g)
plain flour*

*1 teaspoon
bicarbonate of soda*

*1/2 cup (60g) coarsely
chopped walnuts*

*1 cup (190g) dark
Choc Bits*

*1 cup (150g)
milk chocolate
Melts, halved*

*1/3 cup (65g) dark
Choc Bits, extra*

*1/2 cup (75g) milk
chocolate Melts,
quartered, extra*

Beat butter, essence, sugars and eggs in
medium bowl with electric mixer until smooth.
Stir in sifted flour and soda, nuts, Choc Bits and
chocolate Melts; mix well.

Drop level tablespoons of mixture about 5cm
apart on greased oven trays. Press extra Choc
Bits and extra chocolate Melts into cookies.
Bake in moderately hot oven about 12 minutes
or until browned lightly. Stand cookies 2 minutes
before lifting onto wire racks to cool.

Makes about 50

32 anzac biscuits

For a better result, use traditional rolled oats rather than quick-cook rolled oats in this recipe.

1 cup (90g) rolled oats
1 cup (150g) plain flour
1 cup (220g) sugar
3/4 cup (65g) desiccated coconut
125g butter
1 tablespoon golden syrup
1 teaspoon bicarbonate of soda
2 tablespoons boiling water

Combine oats, flour, sugar and coconut in large bowl. Combine butter and golden syrup in small saucepan, stir over heat until butter is melted. Combine soda and water, add to butter mixture; stir into dry ingredients while mixture is still warm.
Place 3 heaped teaspoons of mixture, about 4cm apart on greased oven trays, press biscuits down lightly. Bake in slow oven about 20 minutes or until browned. Stand biscuits 5 minutes, loosen and cool on trays.

Makes about 30

34 the finishing touches

To decorate biscuits and slices is to transform them from pleasingly plain to a sweet, delicious morsel. Try the following ideas to ensure your biscuits and slices realise their full potential.

The most basic decoration for biscuits is a mere dusting of sieved icing sugar, which can be all that some biscuits require. An alternative to this is the use of a soft, flavoured butter icing, a glacé icing – flavoured to suit – a butter cream filling, or melted chocolate, as a dip or spread (suitable for biscuits and slices).

lemon butter icing

1½ cups (240g) icing sugar mixture
20g soft butter
2 tablespoons lemon juice

Combine ingredients in heatproof bowl; stir over hot water until smooth.

tips Change the flavour of this icing by substituting the lemon juice with either orange, lime or mandarin juice, or, for chocolate icing, sift 2 tablespoons cocoa powder into bowl, omitting lemon juice. For vanilla butter icing, add 1 teaspoon vanilla essence to bowl in place of lemon juice.

coconut glacé icing

1 cup (160g) icing sugar mixture
½ teaspoon coconut essence
1½ tablespoons milk, approximately

Place icing sugar in heatproof bowl, stir in essence and enough milk to make a firm paste. Stir over hot water until spreadable.

tips In place of the coconut essence, try using any essence of your choice to flavour the glacé icing, or warm the milk in the recipe and stir in 2 teaspoons of dry instant coffee, until dissolved. You can also omit the flavourings entirely and use food colourings to create a plain icing in the colour of your choice.

chocolate icing

100g dark chocolate, melted
30g unsalted butter, melted

Combine chocolate and butter in small bowl.

tips Dip half of each biscuit into this icing for an attractive look, or spread it onto a slice. For a jaffa-flavoured icing, stir in 2 teaspoons finely grated orange rind.

passionfruit butter cream

60g butter

¾ cup (120g) icing sugar mixture

1 tablespoon passionfruit pulp

2 teaspoons brandy

Beat butter and icing sugar in small bowl with electric mixer until light and fluffy. Stir in passionfruit pulp and brandy.

tips For a delicious mocha butter cream, beat in 1 tablespoon of sifted cocoa powder, and 2 teaspoons of dry instant coffee dissolved in 2 teaspoons of hot water, in place of the passionfruit pulp and brandy. Alternatively, substitute brandy and passionfruit pulp with 1 tablespoon of strawberry topping for a scrumptious, appealing strawberry butter cream.

caramel pistachio
slice

185g butter, melted

2 cups (300g) plain flour

²/₃ cup (150g) caster sugar

1 cup (150g) chopped shelled pistachios, toasted

filling

395g can sweetened condensed milk

60g butter

2 tablespoons golden syrup

¹/₃ cup (80ml) sour cream

Grease 20cm x 30cm lamington pan, line base and two long sides with baking paper, extending paper 2cm above edge of pan.

Combine butter, flour and sugar in large bowl; press over base of prepared pan. Bake in moderate oven about 25 minutes or until browned lightly; cool.

Spread Filling over base; sprinkle with nuts. Cool in pan, before cutting.

Filling Combine milk, butter and syrup in medium saucepan, stir over low heat about 15 minutes or until mixture is thick and caramel in colour. Stir in cream.

corn flake
honey slice

1½ cups (45g)
Corn Flakes

1⅓ cups (120g)
rolled oats

1⅓ cups (120g)
desiccated coconut

¾ cup (165g)
caster sugar

125g butter, melted

2 tablespoons honey

Grease 19cm x 29cm rectangular slice pan.
Combine Corn Flakes, oats, coconut and
sugar in large bowl. Stir in butter and honey;
mix well. Spread into prepared pan; bake
in moderate oven about 20 minutes or until
browned lightly. Stand 15 minutes before
cutting in pan; cool in pan.

lemon
slice

250g packet
malt biscuits

150g butter, melted

1 cup (70g)
shredded coconut

1 tablespoon
lemon butter

2 teaspoons water

lemon curd

6 eggs, beaten lightly

3 teaspoons finely
grated lemon rind

1/2 cup (125ml)
lemon juice

1 cup (220g)
caster sugar

300ml thickened
cream

Grease 20cm x 30cm lamington pan; line base and two long sides with baking paper, extending paper 2cm above edge of pan.

Process biscuits until crushed, transfer to medium bowl; stir in butter and half of the coconut. Press mixture over base of prepared pan, cover; refrigerate 1 hour or until firm. Pour Lemon Curd over base in pan, place pan on oven tray. Bake, in moderate oven about 30 minutes or until set slightly.

Cool in pan, cover; refrigerate until cold. Combine lemon butter and water in small saucepan, stir over low heat until combined; brush over slice, sprinkle with remaining coconut.

Lemon Curd Whisk ingredients together in medium bowl; strain.

40 chocolate brownies

with sour cream frosting

125g butter

185g dark chocolate, chopped

1 cup (220g) caster sugar

2 teaspoons vanilla essence

2 eggs, beaten lightly

1 cup (150g) plain flour

1/2 cup (60g) chopped pecans

sour cream frosting

100g dark chocolate, chopped

1/4 cup (60ml) sour cream

Grease deep 19cm square cake pan, line base and two sides with baking paper, extending paper 2cm above edge of pan.

Melt butter and chocolate in medium heatproof bowl over pan of simmering water. Stir in sugar and essence, then eggs, flour and nuts. Pour mixture into prepared pan; bake in moderate oven about 30 minutes or until just firm. Cool in pan. Turn brownie out; top with Sour Cream Frosting. Cover; refrigerate brownie before cutting.

Sour Cream Frosting Melt chocolate in small heatproof bowl over pan of simmering water, stir in sour cream; stir until mixture is smooth and glossy.

chocolate

coconut rough

1 cup (150g)
self-raising flour

1 tablespoon
cocoa powder

1/3 cup (75g)
caster sugar

1/4 cup (20g)
desiccated coconut

125g butter, melted

**chocolate coconut
topping**

1 cup (160g) icing
sugar mixture

1 tablespoon
cocoa powder

1 cup (90g)
desiccated coconut

1/4 cup (60ml)
sweetened
condensed milk

60g butter, melted

Grease 19cm x 29cm rectangular slice pan.
Sift flour, cocoa and sugar into medium bowl,
stir in coconut and butter. Press over base of
prepared pan; bake in moderate oven about
20 minutes. Stand in pan 5 minutes.
Spread with Chocolate Coconut Topping;
roughen topping with a fork. Cover;
refrigerate until cold before cutting.
Chocolate Coconut Topping Sift icing sugar
and cocoa into a medium bowl; stir in coconut,
then milk and butter.

lemon sunburst

1 cup (150g) self-raising flour

1 1/4 cups (185g) plain flour

2 cups (320g) icing sugar mixture

250g butter, chopped

4 eggs

1 1/2 cups (330g) caster sugar

1 tablespoon finely grated lemon rind

1/2 cup (125ml) lemon juice

Grease 20cm x 30cm lamington pan, line base and two long sides with baking paper, extending paper 2cm above edge of pan.

Process self-raising flour, 1 cup of the plain flour, 1/2 cup of the icing sugar and butter until combined. Press over base of prepared pan; bake in moderate oven about 20 minutes, or until firm. Cool in pan.

Whisk eggs, caster sugar, remaining plain flour, rind and 1/4 cup of the juice in medium bowl; pour over biscuit base. Bake in moderate oven about 30 minutes, or until firm; cool in pan.

Stir remaining icing sugar and remaining juice in small bowl until smooth; spread over slice, cut when set.

chocolate fruit slice

125g butter

1 cup (150g)
self-raising flour

2 tablespoons
cocoa powder

1/2 cup (110g)
caster sugar

1 cup (90g)
desiccated coconut

1/2 cup (95g) dried
mixed fruit

1/4 cup (30g)
chopped pecans

2 tablespoons
desiccated
coconut, extra

chocolate icing

1 1/2 cups (240g) icing
sugar mixture

1/4 cup (25g)
cocoa powder

2 teaspoons
melted butter

2 tablespoons milk,
approximately

Grease 19cm x 29cm rectangular slice pan,
line base and two long sides with baking paper,
extending paper 2cm above edge of pan.
Melt butter in medium saucepan, remove from
heat. Stir in sifted flour and cocoa, sugar,
coconut, dried fruit and nuts; press over base
of prepared pan. Bake in moderate oven about
20 minutes or until firm. Spread with Chocolate
Icing, sprinkle with extra coconut. Cool in pan,
before cutting.

Chocolate Icing Sift icing sugar and cocoa
into medium bowl, stir in butter and enough
milk to make a stiff paste.

peanut
slice

1½ cups (225g) plain flour

125g butter

1 tablespoon water, approximately

¼ cup (110g) raspberry jam

topping

1 egg white

¾ cup (165g) caster sugar

½ cup (50g) cake crumbs

1 tablespoon cocoa powder

1½ cups (250g) unsalted roasted peanuts

1 teaspoon vanilla essence

Grease 19cm x 29cm lamington pan.
Place flour in medium bowl; rub in butter. Add enough water to make ingredients cling together. Knead gently on floured surface until smooth. Cover pastry; refrigerate 30 minutes.

Roll out pastry until large enough to cover base of prepared pan; prick well with fork. Bake in moderate oven 15 minutes; cool 10 minutes. Spread evenly with jam, then Topping. Brush surface evenly with water. Bake in moderate oven for about 20 minutes, or until lightly browned. Cool in pan before cutting.
Topping Beat egg white in small bowl until stiff, add sugar, beat 1 minute; fold in cake crumbs, cocoa, peanuts and essence.

tangy apricot slice

125g butter

¼ cup (60ml) honey

¼ cup (50g)
brown sugar

12 (200g) Weet-Bix,
crushed finely

2⅔ cups (400g)
dried apricots

½ cup (110g)
caster sugar

1 cup (90g)
desiccated coconut

1⅓ cups (200g)
white chocolate
Melts, melted

Grease 19cm x 29cm rectangular slice pan, line base and two long sides with baking paper, extending paper 2cm above edge of pan.
Combine butter, honey and brown sugar in medium saucepan; stir over heat until sugar dissolves. Stir in Weet-Bix crumbs, press over base of prepared pan.
Place apricots in medium heatproof bowl, cover with boiling water, stand 5 minutes. Drain apricots; discard liquid. Process apricots until pureed; add caster sugar and coconut, process until combined. With the motor operating, add chocolate in a thin stream. Spread apricot mixture over crumb layer in pan. Cover, refrigerate until firm before cutting.

date and **lemon** slice

1 cup (150g)
self-raising flour

1 cup (90g) rolled oats

1/2 cup (55g)
hazelnut meal

1/2 cup (100g) firmly
packed brown sugar

125g butter, melted

1 egg, beaten lightly

topping

11/2 cups (240g)
chopped seeded dates

1/2 cup (125ml) water

1/4 cup (60ml)
lemon juice

2 tablespoons
golden syrup

1/2 cup (60g) chopped
roasted hazelnuts

1/4 cup (20g)
rolled oats

Grease 19cm x 29cm rectangular slice pan, line base and two long sides with baking paper, extending paper 2cm above edge of pan.
Combine ingredients in medium bowl; press into prepared pan. Bake in moderate oven 15 minutes. Cool 5 minutes; spread with

Topping. Bake in moderate oven about 25 minutes or until firm. Cool in pan, before cutting.
Topping Combine dates, water, juice and golden syrup in medium saucepan; simmer, uncovered, until mixture is thick. Stir in nuts and oats; cool 10 minutes.

peanut **bubble** bars

125g butter

1/3 cup (80ml) light corn syrup

1/3 cup (85g) smooth peanut butter

1/2 cup (110g) caster sugar

2 cups (70g) Rice Bubbles

2 cups (90g) Coco Pops

1 cup (80g) flaked almonds, toasted

Grease 20cm x 30cm lamington pan, line base and two long sides with baking paper, extending paper 2cm above edge of pan.

Combine butter, corn syrup, peanut butter and sugar in medium saucepan; stir over heat, without boiling, until sugar dissolves. Bring to boil; simmer gently, uncovered, without stirring, 5 minutes. Gently stir in remaining ingredients; press mixture into prepared pan. Cover; refrigerate before cutting.

hazelnut, fig
and ricotta slice

100g butter, chopped

1/3 cup (75g) firmly
packed brown sugar

1 egg

1 cup (150g)
self-raising flour

1/2 cup (75g) plain flour

1/2 cup (55g)
hazelnut meal

filling

400g ricotta cheese

1/2 cup (110g)
caster sugar

1/2 cup (60g) chopped
roasted hazelnuts

2 tablespoons
Frangelico

1/4 cup (45g) chopped
dried figs

Grease 20cm x 30cm lamington pan.
Process ingredients until crumbly; do not
over-process. Press half the mixture over base
of prepared pan. Pour Filling over base; sprinkle
with remaining base mixture. Bake in moderate
oven about 45 minutes or until slice is firm.
Cool in pan, before cutting.
Filling Combine ingredients in medium bowl;
mix well.

apricot glazed

butterscotch slice

100g butter

¾ cup (150g) firmly packed brown sugar

2 tablespoons cream

1 cup (150g) plain flour

1 egg, beaten lightly

⅓ cup (55g) whole blanched almonds

2 tablespoons apricot jam, warmed

Grease 19cm x 29cm rectangular slice pan, line base and two long sides with baking paper, extending paper 2cm above edge of pan.
Combine butter, sugar and cream in medium saucepan; stir over heat, without boiling, until sugar dissolves. Boil, uncovered, without stirring, about 3 minutes or until mixture becomes darker in colour, cool 10 minutes.
Stir flour and egg into mixture; spread into prepared pan, top with nuts. Bake in moderate oven about 20 minutes or until just firm. Brush warm slice with jam. Cool in pan, before cutting.

52 hazelnut fudge
temptation

250g packet plain
sweet biscuits

1/3 cup (35g) hazelnut meal

125g butter, melted

40g butter, extra

1 cup (150g) milk
chocolate Melts

395g can sweetened
condensed milk

1/4 cup (60ml) Nutella

1/2 cup (75g) roasted
hazelnuts, chopped

Grease 20cm x 30cm lamington pan,
line base and two long sides with
baking paper, extending paper 2cm
above edge of pan.
Process biscuits to fine crumbs, add
hazelnut meal and butter, process
until combined. Press over base of
prepared pan. Combine extra butter,
chocolate Melts, milk and Nutella in
medium pan; stir over low heat until
butter and chocolate melts and mixture
thickens. Stir in nuts, spread over
crumb layer. Cover; refrigerate until
set, before cutting.

double

bubble snack

2 cups (70g) Rice Bubbles

2 cups (90g) Coco Pops

*1 cup (70g)
shredded coconut*

125g butter, chopped

1/3 cup (80ml) honey

*1/3 cup (85g) smooth
peanut butter*

1/2 cup (110g) caster sugar

Grease 20cm x 30cm lamington pan; line base and two long sides with baking paper, extending paper 2cm above edge of pan.

Combine Rice Bubbles, Coco Pops and coconut in large bowl. Combine remaining ingredients in small saucepan; stir over heat, without boiling, until sugar dissolves, then simmer, uncovered, without stirring, 5 minutes. Add sugar mixture to cereal mixture; mix gently, press firmly over base of prepared pan. Cover; refrigerate until firm, before cutting.

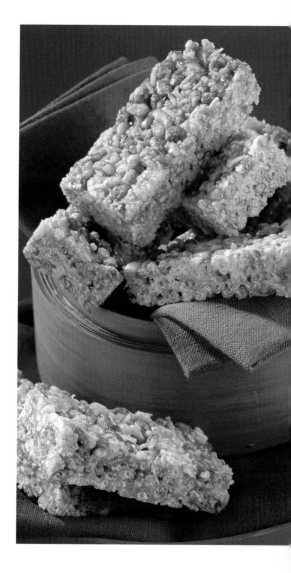

185g butter

1/3 cup (80ml) honey

3/4 cup (90g) instant malted milk powder

2 cups (70g) Rice Bubbles

2 cups (60g) Corn Flakes

1 cup (100g) plain cake crumbs

1/2 cup (45g) desiccated coconut

1/2 cup (40g) flaked almonds, toasted

Grease 20cm x 30cm lamington pan, line base and two long sides with baking paper, extending paper 2cm above edge of pan. **Combine** butter, honey and milk powder in medium saucepan; stir over heat, until butter is melted. Remove pan from heat, stir in remaining ingredients; press mixture firmly into prepared pan. Cover, refrigerate before cutting.

raspberry almond slice 55

1 cup (150g)
self-raising flour

1 cup (150g)
plain flour

1½ cups (300g) firmly
packed brown sugar

125g butter, chopped

1 teaspoon
bicarbonate of soda

¾ cup (180ml)
buttermilk

1 egg, beaten lightly

2 teaspoons finely
grated lemon rind

125g fresh or
frozen raspberries

¼ cup (20g)
flaked almonds

Grease 20cm x 30cm lamington pan.
Process flours, sugar and butter until mixture is
fine. Press 2 cups of the mixture over base of
prepared pan. Place remaining mixture in
medium bowl, stir in soda, buttermilk, egg
and rind. Pour over base, top with berries,
sprinkle with nuts.
Bake in moderate oven about 35 minutes or
until firm. Cool in pan, before cutting.

SAIT - Library

almond slice

125g butter

1/4 cup (55g) caster sugar

1 cup (150g) plain flour

90g butter, extra

1 tablespoon finely grated orange rind

1/3 cup (75g) caster sugar, extra

2 eggs

1 1/2 cups (185g) almond meal

1/2 cup (40g) flaked almonds

1/4 cup (60ml) apricot jam

Grease 19cm x 29cm rectangular slice pan, line base and two long sides with baking paper, extending paper 2cm above edge of pan. **Beat** butter and sugar in small bowl with electric mixer until light and fluffy. Stir in flour in two batches; spread into prepared pan. **Beat** extra butter, rind and extra sugar in small bowl with electric mixer until just combined. Add eggs, beat until combined, (mixture may curdle). Stir in almond meal; spread over base in pan. Sprinkle with nuts; bake in moderate oven about 20 minutes or until browned lightly. Brush gently with warm strained apricot jam. Cool in pan, before cutting.

coconut apple
crumble slice

100g butter

1/2 cup (110g)
caster sugar

1 cup (150g)
plain flour

3/4 cup (65g)
desiccated coconut

1 1/4 cups canned
pie apples

topping

1/2 cup (75g) plain flour

1 teaspoon
ground cinnamon

30g butter

1/4 cup (55g)
caster sugar

Grease 20cm x 30cm lamington pan.
Beat butter and sugar in small bowl with electric
mixer until light and fluffy. Stir in flour and
coconut. Press mixture evenly over base of
prepared pan; bake in moderately hot oven
about 12 minutes or until browned lightly, cool.
Spread base with apple, sprinkle with Topping;
bake in moderate oven about 35 minutes or until
browned lightly. Cool in pan, before cutting.
Topping Combine flour and cinnamon in medium
bowl, rub in butter; stir in sugar.

easy
muesli slice

½ cup (125ml) honey

½ cup (130g)
peanut butter

¾ cup (120g)
wholemeal
self-raising flour

¾ cup (65g)
rolled oats

¼ cup (10g)
flaked coconut

⅓ cup (40g)
finely chopped
roasted hazelnuts

½ cup (80g) sultanas

¼ cup (35g)
finely chopped
dried apricots

¼ cup (20g) finely
chopped dried apples

¼ cup (50g) seeded
finely chopped prunes

2 tablespoons
sunflower
seed kernels

1 tablespoon
sesame seeds

2 eggs, beaten lightly

Grease 19cm x 29cm rectangular slice pan, line base and two long sides with baking paper, extending paper 2cm above edge of pan.
Stir honey and peanut butter in medium saucepan over heat until combined; remove from heat, stir in remaining ingredients.
Spread over base of prepared pan; bake in moderate oven about 20 minutes. Cool in pan, before cutting.

200g dark chocolate, melted

90g butter, melted

4 cups (400g) chocolate cake crumbs

2 tablespoons Irish cream liqueur

1 cup (125g) chopped roasted hazelnuts

creamy chocolate frosting

1/4 cup (60ml) cream

50g dark chocolate

30g butter

1 cup (160g) icing sugar mixture

Grease 19cm x 29cm rectangular slice pan, line base and two long sides with baking paper, extending paper 2cm above edge of pan. **Combine** chocolate and butter in medium bowl; stir in crumbs, liqueur and nuts. Press over base of prepared pan; cover, refrigerate until set. Spread with Creamy Chocolate Frosting.

Creamy Chocolate Frosting Heat cream in small saucepan until almost boiling. Transfer cream to medium bowl, add chocolate and butter, stir until smooth. Gradually beat in icing sugar, cover; refrigerate 10 minutes, stirring occasionally, until a spreading consistency.

glossary

almond meal almonds ground to a flour-like texture; also known as finely ground almonds.

baking powder a raising agent consisting mainly of 2 parts cream of tartar to 1 part bicarbonate of soda (baking soda).

banana chips sliced dried bananas.

bicarbonate of soda also known as baking soda.

biscuits

malt: malt-flavoured uniced packaged biscuit.

plain sweet: uniced and unfilled plain packaged biscuit.

buttermilk low-fat milk cultured to give a slightly sour, tangy taste; low-fat yogurt can be substituted.

cheese

cream: also known as "Philadelphia"; a soft milk cheese with no less than 33% butterfat.

ricotta: a fresh, unripened cheese made from whey.

Cherry Ripe bars made from chocolate, coconut, sugar, cherries glucose and milk powder.

chocolate Choc bits: also known as chocolate chips and chocolate morsels; available in milk, white and dark chocolate. Made of cocoa liquor, cocoa butter, sugar and an emulsifier, these hold their shape in baking and are ideal for decorating.

coated honeycomb bars: chocolate-dipped honeycomb; made from chocolate, sugar, glucose and gelatine. We used Violet Crumble.

Melts: available in milk, white and dark chocolate. Made from sugar, vegetable fats, milk solids, cocoa powder, butter oil and emulsifiers, these are good for melting and moulding.

coconut

desiccated: unsweetened, concentrated, dried shredded coconut.

flaked: flaked and dried coconut flesh.

shredded: thin strips of dried coconut flesh.

Coco Pops chocolate-flavoured puffed rice eaten as breakfast cereal.

cornflour also known as cornstarch.

corn syrup an imported product. It is available in light or dark colour; either can be substituted for the other. Glucose syrup (liquid glucose) can be substituted.

cream

cream: regular pouring cream.

sour: a thick, commercially cultured soured cream (minimum fat content 35%), good for dips, toppings and baked cheesecakes.

thickened: a whipping cream (minimum fat content 35%) containing a thickener.

custard powder packaged, vanilla pudding mixture.

eggs some recipes in this book call for raw or barely cooked eggs; exercise caution if there is a salmonella problem in your area.

essence also known as extract; generally the by-product of distillation of plants.

flour

rice: a very fine flour, made from ground white rice.

white plain: an all-purpose flour, made from wheat.

white self-raising: plain flour sifted with baking powder in the proportion of 1 cup flour to 2 teaspoons baking powder.

wholemeal plain: also known as all-purpose wholewheat flour; add baking powder as above to make wholemeal self-raising flour.

Frangelico hazelnut-flavoured liqueur.

golden syrup maple syrup or honey can be substituted. Do not use the golden syrup available in squeeze bottles as results will vary.

hazelnut meal we used packaged, commercially ground nuts.

Irish Cream we used Baileys Original Irish Cream, based on Irish whiskey, spirits and cream.

jam also known as preserves or conserve; most often made from fruit.

lemon butter lemon curd or lemon cheese.

malted milk powder instant powdered product made from cow's milk, extracts of malted barley and other cereals.

maple-flavoured syrup also known as pancake syrup but not a substitute for pure maple syrup.

mixed spice a blend of ground spices usually consisting of cinnamon, allspice and nutmeg.

Nutella chocolate hazelnut spread.

oil

vegetable: any of a number of oils sourced from plants rather than animal fats.

orange flower water concentrated flavouring that is made from orange blossoms.

pepitas dried and hulled pumpkin seeds.

pine nuts small, cream-coloured kernels from the cones of various pine trees.

Rice Bubbles rice crispies.

rolled oats whole oat grains that are steamed and flattened, then dried and packaged for consumption.

rum liquor made from fermented sugarcane; available in dark or light varieties.

Dark: we prefer to use an underproof rum (not overproof) for a more subtle flavour.

sugar we used coarse, granulated table sugar, also known as crystal sugar, unless otherwise specified.

brown: an extremely soft, fine granulated sugar retaining molasses for its characteristic colour and flavour.

caster: also known as superfine or finely granulated table sugar.

icing sugar mixture: also known as confectioners' sugar or powdered sugar; granulated sugar crushed together with a small amount (about 3%) cornflour added.

raw: natural brown granulated sugar.

sweetened condensed milk we used Nestlé's milk which has had 60% of the water removed, then sweetened with sugar.

yogurt-coated sultanas sultanas covered in a sweetened yogurt coating.

facts and figures

These conversions are approximate only, but the difference between an exact and the approximate conversion of various liquid and dry measures is minimal and will not affect your cooking results.

Measuring equipment

The difference between one country's measuring cups and another's is, at most, within a 2 or 3 teaspoon variance. (For the record, 1 Australian metric measuring cup holds approximately 250ml.) The most accurate way of measuring dry ingredients is to weigh them. For liquids, use a clear glass or plastic jug having metric markings.

Note: NZ, Canada, USA and UK all use 15ml tablespoons. Australian tablespoons measure 20ml.
All cup and spoon measurements are level.

How to measure

When using graduated measuring cups, shake dry ingredients loosely into the appropriate cup. Do not tap the cup on a bench or tightly pack the ingredients unless directed to do so. Level the top of measuring cups and measuring spoons with a knife. When measuring liquids, place a clear glass or plastic jug having metric markings on a flat surface to check accuracy at eye level.

Dry Measures

metric	imperial
15g	1/2oz
30g	1oz
60g	2oz
90g	3oz
125g	4oz (1/4lb)
155g	5oz
185g	6oz
220g	7oz
250g	8oz (1/2lb)
280g	9oz
315g	10oz
345g	11oz
375g	12oz (3/4lb)
410g	13oz
440g	14oz
470g	15oz
500g	16oz (1lb)
750g	24oz (11/2lb)
1kg	32oz (2lb)

We use large eggs having an average weight of 60g.

Liquid Measures

metric	imperial
30ml	1 fluid oz
60ml	2 fluid oz
100ml	3 fluid oz
125ml	4 fluid oz
150ml	5 fluid oz (1/4 pint/1 gill)
190ml	6 fluid oz
250ml (1cup)	8 fluid oz
300ml	10 fluid oz (1/2 pint)
500ml	16 fluid oz
600ml	20 fluid oz (1 pint)
1000ml (1litre)	1 3/4 pints

Helpful Measures

metric	imperial
3mm	1/8in
6mm	1/4in
1cm	1/2in
2cm	3/4in
2.5cm	1in
6cm	21/2in
8cm	3in
20cm	8in
23cm	9in
25cm	10in
30cm	12in (1ft)

Oven Temperatures

These oven temperatures are only a guide.
Always check the manufacturer's manual.

	°C (Celsius)	°F (Fahrenheit)	Gas Mark
Very slow	120	250	1
Slow	150	300	2
Moderately slow	160	325	3
Moderate	180 –190	350 – 375	4
Moderately hot	200 – 210	400 – 425	5
Hot	220 – 230	450 – 475	6
Very hot	240 – 250	500 – 525	7

Food editor Pamela Clark
Associate food editor Karen Hammial
Assistant food editor Kathy McGarry
Assistant recipe editor Elizabeth Hooper

HOME LIBRARY STAFF
Editor-in-chief Mary Coleman
Managing editor (food) Susan Tomnay
Marketing manager Nicole Pizanis
Editor Julie Collard
Concept design Jackie Richards
Designer Mary Keep
Group publisher Jill Baker
Chief executive officer John Alexander

Produced by *The Australian Women's Weekly*
Home Library, Sydney.

Colour separations by
ACP Colour Graphics Pty Ltd, Sydney.
Printing by Dai Nippon Printing, Korea.

Published by ACP Publishing Pty Limited,
54 Park Street, Sydney; GPO Box 4088, Sydney,
NSW 1028. Ph: (02) 9282 8618
Fax: (02) 9267 9438.

AWWHomeLib@publishing.acp.com.au

Australia Distributed by Network Distribution
Company, GPO Box 4088, Sydney, NSW 1028.
Ph: (02) 9282 8777 Fax: (02) 9264 3278.

United Kingdom Distributed by Australian
Consolidated Press (UK), Moulton Park Business
Centre, Red House Road, Moulton Park,
Northampton, NN3 6AQ. Ph: (01604) 497 531
Fax: (01604) 497 533 Acpukltd@aol.com

Canada Distributed by Whitecap Books Ltd,
351 Lynn Ave, North Vancouver, BC, V7J 2C4,
(604) 980 9852.

New Zealand Distributed by Netlink Distribution
Company, Level 4, 23 Hargreaves St,
College Hill, Auckland 1, (9) 302 7616.

South Africa Distributed by PSD Promotions
(Pty) Ltd,PO Box 1175, Isando 1600, SA,
(011) 392 6065.
CNA Limited, Newsstand Division, PO Box 10799,
Johannesburg 2000. Ph (011) 491 7500.

Sweet and Simple: Biscuits and Slices.

Includes index.
ISBN 1 86396 182 8.

1. Cookies. I. Title: Australian Women's Weekly.
(Series: Australian Women's Weekly sweet
and simple mini series).
641.8654

© ACP Publishing Pty Limited 2000
ACN 053 273 546

Cover Vanilla currant cookies, page 22
Stylist Sarah O'Brien
Photographer Scott Cameron
Home economist Karen Green
Back cover Double heart biscuits, page 23

The publishers would like to thank: The Bay Tree
Kitchen Shop, Woollahra, NSW; Victoria Spring
Designs, Paddington, NSW; and Grace Bros for
additional props used in photography.

mini books